MEMORIES
OF THE
WREKIN
AND BEYOND

ALTON DOUGLAS

DENNIS MOORE

ADDITIONAL RESEARCH BY JO DOUGLAS

ISBN 0 947865 07 1
Published by Beacon Broadcasting Ltd., 267 Tettenhall Road, Wolverhampton, WV6 0DQ.
Printed by Windmill Printing, Portersfield Road, Cradley Heath, Warley, West Midlands, B64 7BX.
Layout by Alton and Jo Douglas.

Ironbridge, 1975.

Front cover: Madeley, from the tower of St Michael's Church, June 1977.

Page one: Wellington, looking towards The Square, June 1953.

CONTENTS

INTRODUCTION

"All round the Wrekin!" has been a Shropshire toast from time immemorial, yet this hearty and convivial sentiment seems unchanged by time and never out of place.

The Wrekin rises suddenly from the Shropshire plain to a height of 1,335 feet (407 metres) above mean sea-level and is said to be the highest hill in Europe for the circumference of its base. Its name is derived from "wre" and "ken", two Celtic terms meaning "principal or most conspicuous hill". From any point for miles around it is the chief feature of the landscape. Viewed from the north-west it appears like some stranded creature from the depths of the ocean; whilst from the south-east its rainbow shape has the appearance of a stupendous arch of Nature's making. The views from the summit are breathtaking. On a clear day, particularly just after a rainstorm when the air has been cleared of dust and smoke, 17 old-style counties can be seen, Leicester, Derby and Oxford being at the extreme limits. The walk to the top is not arduous, given frequent stops for refreshment or to take in the view.

During the Second World War, the Wrekin's red, winking beacon (which warned aviators of high ground), flashed continuously throughout the conflict, being considered of more value to friend than to foe.

Approaching the top, the walker will pass through narrow gaps called Hell Gate and Heaven Gate, ancient entrances to a long-lost Iron Age fort. Legend has it that two giants fought here. One struck at the other with a spade, missed and split a nearby rock, creating the Needle's Eye. A raven proceeded to peck at this giant's eyes, he wept and his tears fell to form the pool known as the Raven's Pool. Legends of the Wrekin are plentiful. Another giant once quarrelled with the good folk of Shrewsbury and set off with a huge spadeful of earth to bury the whole town. On the way he met a cobbler carrying a sack full of shoes to be mended. The cobbler persuaded the giant that Shrewsbury was too far to walk, proving his case by showing him the bag of shoes he had worn out on the long and arduous journey from the town. The giant was convinced, dropped the mighty spadeful of earth, forming the Wrekin and his little brother, the Ercall.

Looking at the green, well-wooded countryside surrounding the hill, it seems difficult, sometimes, to appreciate that the region was once so industrialised. At Coalbrookdale, in 1709, Abraham Darby began to smelt iron-ore, using coke in place of the traditional charcoal: The Industrial Revolution was born. Darby's historic furnace is still there and can be viewed in its own special building. In 1777 Darby's grandson, another Abraham, cast the massive ribs for the world's first iron bridge, opened in 1779 and the Ironbridge Gorge had become one of the world's major iron centres. The Ironbridge Gorge Museum is now a prime tourist attraction.

A little farther, at Tong near Shifnal, the parish church of St. Bartholomew has been described as "The Cathedral of the West Midlands" because of its design and setting. It was here that Charles Dickens placed the last chapters of his novel "The Old Curiosity Shop" and has the character of Little Nell buried. An early, enterprising verger marked out a plot in the churchyard, now headed "The Reputed Grave of Little Nell", hoping to gain a fair income from conducting visitors to it. He even forged an entry in the burial register to give authority to his claim! The grave remains to this day.

The Wrekin has seen a great deal over the years: industrial changes, powered flight, motorways, telecommunications and New Towns. Doubtless the world will continue to change at a terrifying speed but, through it all, the Wrekin remains as reassuringly imperturbable as ever. What was that toast again? "All round the Wrekin!" Cheers!

WE'VE GOT YOU COVERED SHROPSHIRE

July 1987

BEACON RADIO is not in the business of 'pop music and prattle' - so says Alan Mullett, the station's no-nonsense, Wolverhampton-born managing director now living in Shropshire.

Beacon prides itself on being entertaining and informative and closely attuned to the broadcasting needs of the communities it serves.

Since July 14 the station has extended its service from the West Midlands and the Black Country to Shropshire where its Wrekin transmitter can reach an extra 172,000 people.

Initially, Shropshire will get its own programmes from 6 a.m. to 10 a.m. with *Beacon* having news and interview facilities in both Shrewsbury and Telford.

Exciting time

Local news and sport will form a major part of the *Beacon* Shropshire output with the audience also having the benefit of popular *Beacon* Wolverhampton features such as 'Helpline' — a lifeline for the community (see page 2) — and regular competitions.

"Our general programming and output certainly reflect the fact that Shropshire is now an important audience for us," said Alan.

"It's an exciting time for us, our advertisers and our listeners. We actively encourage our listeners to telephone us — part of our positive commitment to be close to the community we serve."

Local

In fact, *Beacon* has 25 telephone lines and with features such as 'Helpline,' 'Voteline,' 'Celebration Line' and numerous competitions and phone-ins, there is almost constant dialogue between the station and its listeners.

"Our major strength is being 'local' and actively communicating with people. Beacon is part of the community — without that two-way commitment between radio and its listeners, we simply wouldn't be able to exist.

"We have a history of providing entertaining radio for our audience — it's a successful formula which we are continuing for all our listeners in Shropshire the West Midlands, and the Black Country."

Alan Mullett

3

BEGINNINGS

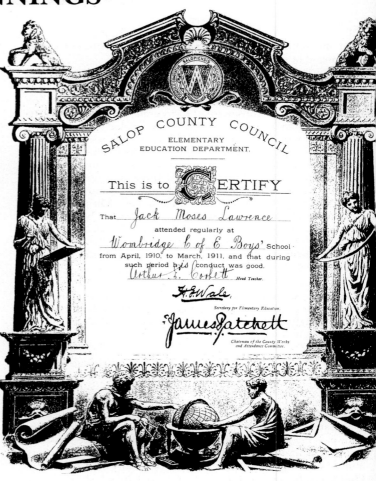

SALOP COUNTY COUNCIL
ELEMENTARY EDUCATION DEPARTMENT.

This is to CERTIFY

That *Jack Moses Lawrence* attended regularly at *Wombridge C of E Boys'* School from April, 1910, to March, 1911, and that during such period *his* conduct was good.

Arthur E. Corbett Head Teacher.

H. J. Wale, Secretary for Elementary Education.

James Patchett Chairman of the County Works and Attendance Committee.

EA 730170

FORM of CERTIFICATE of REGISTRY of BIRTH or STILLBIRTH
BIRTHS AND DEATHS REGISTRATION ACT, 1874, SECTION 30.

I, the undersigned, Do hereby certify that the Birth of a *male* child born on the *3rd March* 1936 has been duly registered by me at Entry No. *1* of my Register Book No. *155*

Name of informant *Albert Rhode Shenton*

Qualifications of informant *Father*

Witness my hand, this *9th* day of *April* 1936

William Edge { Registrar of Births and Deaths.

District *Wenlock* Sub-District *Madeley*

Caution.—Any person who (1) falsifies any of the particulars on this certificate, or (2) uses it as true, knowing it to be false, is liable to Prosecution.

Grade 4, Wombridge Junior School, 1934.

St Leonard's Infants' School, Bridgnorth, 1935.

The Hiatt College, Wellington, 1938.

A bewildered group of boys from Holly Lodge High School, in Smethwick, arrive at Newport Station, 1st September 1939. Virtually the whole school was evacuated just two days before war broke out. On arrival they were served cool drinks by the WVS and Red Cross, a very welcome thought as it was one of the hottest days of the year.

Ellerdine County School, 1940. The school closed finally in July 1992.

Bridgnorth Grammar School, 1946.

Nativity Play, St Leonard's Church,
Bridgnorth, Christmas 1944.

Wombridge Primary School, 1952.

Christmas party-time at Ketley County School, (now Ketley County Infants' School), 1953.

Form IVs, Wellington High School for Girls, at their picnic site, near Hawkstone Park, July 1954.

Pool Hill School Choir, Dawley, 1956.

A school visit to the Creamery, Crudgington, c. 1959.

Dothill Junior School, Wellington, 1967.

IN WHICH THEY SERVE

Wellington Fire Brigade and its fire engine, attract a lot of attention, c. 1900.

Staff of the Officers' Mess, RAF Shawbury, 29th March 1919.

Oakengates Salvation Army Young People's Band, 1929.

S.A.Y.P. Band

Teaching Staff, Wombridge School, 1934.

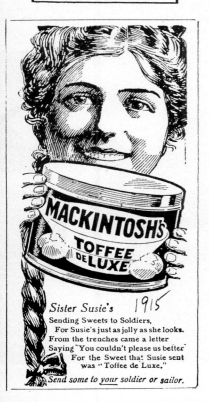

Two United States Air Force NCO's of 309th Pursuit Squadron get to grips with British "Bobbies" bicycles, High Ercall, June 1942.

One of this book's authors, Dennis Moore (left), a Flying Officer navigator, is seen here with his pilot, Flying Officer John Ayre, at 60 OTU, RAF High Ercall, in front of their Mosquito Mk. VI, September 1944. They went on to complete 26 operational flights by the end of the war in Europe.

A Stirling and crew from Central Navigation School, Shawbury on return from navigation exercises to Jan Mayen Island in the Arctic, August 1944.

THIS CERTIFICATE OF HONOUR

IS AWARDED TO

Wombridge Junior School

SAVINGS GROUP

IN RECOGNITION OF SPECIAL ACHIEVEMENT
DURING THE

WINGS FOR VICTORY

NATIONAL SAVINGS CAMPAIGN 1943

I EXTEND MY THANKS TO ALL CONCERNED
IN THIS IMPORTANT NATIONAL SERVICE.

Archibald Sinclair

SECRETARY OF STATE FOR AIR

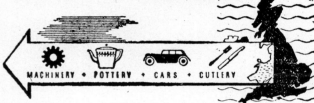
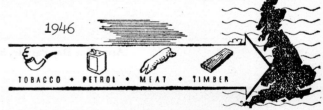

Armistice Day Parade, St Nicholas Church, Newport, 1951.

Red Cross Cadets, Newport, 1951.

West Mercia Constabulary, 'G' Division - on amalgamation, Wellington, September 1967.

Wellington and District Brownies' Thinking Day, 20th February 1970.

16

Armistice Day Parade, High Street, Dawley, c. 1975.

Elected Members and Officers of Wrekin District Council, first AGM, 1974.

2497 (Cosford) ATC Squadron take part in the Broseley Carnival, 1976.

Opening Day, Malinsgate Police Station, Telford, 16th April 1985.

EVENTS

Mr Hamel's Blériot monoplane at Hinstock Show, 18th July 1912.

After the fire at Groom's Wood Yard, Wellington, 16th July 1924.

Retirement party held for Mr T. W. Head, retiring Managing Director of H. & M. Southwell Ltd., The Friars, Bridgnorth, 3rd August 1929.

Celebrating the Coronation of King George VI,
St Leonard's Church, Bridgnorth, 1937.

Lord Bradford, with Lady Anne, crowns the May
Queen, Weston Village Hall, 1937.

St. Leonard's Church Festival, Bridgnorth, Summer 1942.

Princess Elizabeth talks to Mr J. H. Matthews, Sales Director, Merrythought Toy Manufacturers, of Ironbridge, at the British Industries Fair, 1951.

Bridgnorth Grammar School

peech Day & Distribution of Prizes

BY

Mr. J. F. WOLFENDEN, M.A.

(Headmaster of Shrewsbury).

IN THE SCHOOL HALL, on

Thursday, 14th December, 1944,

At 2-30 p.m.

x-roast, Northgate, Bridgnorth, 2nd ne 1953. The event was to celebrate e Coronation of Queen Elizabeth II.

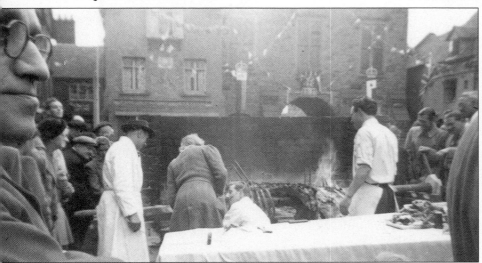

MESSAGE FROM K.S.L.I.'s COLONEL-IN-CHIEF

MAJOR-GENERAL J. M. L. GROVER, C.B., M.C. (Colonel of the King's Shropshire Light Infantry) has sent the following letter to the Lord Lieutenant of Shropshire (Major-General The Viscount Bridgeman, K.B.E., C.B., D.S.O., M.C.) in reply to one sent by the Lord Lieutenant following the presentation of New Colours to the First Battalion at Gottingen on the 15th October, 1954:

"I am writing, on behalf of all ranks of the King's Shropshire Light Infantry, to thank you most warmly for your letter of the 20th October, 1954, and for your very kind remarks about the ceremony for the Presentation of New Colours to the 1st Battalion of the Regiment by the Chief of the Imperial General Staff, which took place in Germany on the 15th October. I shall be very pleased and proud to convey your own and the County's congratulations to Lt.-Col. P. de C. Jones and all ranks of the 1st Battalion.

"I should like to take this opportunity of expressing the great pride and appreciation which all past and present members of the Regiment felt at the wonderful support given to the Regiment on that occasion.

"It was for us a particular honour that you, as Her Majesty's Lieutenant for Salop, Sir Offley Wakeman, as Chairman of the County Council, and other distinguished members of the County should have made the long journey to Gottingen solely to show the County's interest in the County Regiment, and to share in what to us was a great County and family occasion.

"We now look forward to the opportunity, which I hope may occur next year, when the Regiment may be able to celebrate its Bi-centenary anniversary by the laying up of our old 1st Battalion Colours in St. Chad's Church in Shrewsbury."

29.10.54

MISS PAT HILL, aged 21 newly elected Much Wenlock Carnival Queen. 1959

Presentation to Mr E. G. Head, Departmental Manager, Southwell's Carpet Factory, Bridgnorth, on the occasion of his retirement, 1959.

WHIRLWIND UPROOTS TREES AND KILLS FOWL

1962

TREES were uprooted, fowl pens were smashed and electric cables ripped down by flying branches when a whirlwind hit the Lyre, near Morville, following a violent thunderstorm on Saturday afternoon. A house was also damaged.

The whirlwind struck at 2.55pm, sweeping along the ground, flattening and destroying practically everything in its way. Damage was most severe at the Lye Farm, where about 15 good-sized apple trees in an orchard were completely uprooted.

The opening of the WVS (now WRVS) premises in the grounds of the Walker Technical College, Oakengates, 16th November 1963.

MOTEC 1 was officially opened by Royal Highness The Princess Anne Wednesday, September 10th before representative gathering of guests from many sectors of road transport, education and other authorities.

The Princess, in declaring this Multi-Occupational Training Centre the Road Transport Industry Training Board officially open, unveiled a commemorative Steering Wheel of stainless steel set in the centre island in front Ercall House.

In thanking Her Royal Highness, the Chairman of the Board, Mr. K. C. Turner, C.B.E., said that a lot of hard work had been undertaken in a very short time to set up the Training Centre she was about to see. double-decker around section of MOTEC Her competent hand of the 79-seater public service vehicle won preciative comm from the many onlookers — guests, pressmen and staff alike.

10.9.69

ENTERTAINERS

JOANNE MICHELLE	Soprano of Radio, T.V. & London Cabaret
BARRY BURTON	Comedy Entertainer
ARONWY	Magical Entertainer
BRIAN MALCOLM	Musical Entertainer
ALBERT TINKLER	Accompanist

The Queen leaves the home of Mr and Mrs Dawes, accompanied by Sir Reginald Pearson (DDC Chairman), during her visit to Sutton Hill, 17th March 1967.

The Duke of Edinburgh shares a joke with Dr Tony Trafford, MP for The Wrekin, on the occasion of the opening of the Madeley Court Centre, 14th July 1972.

Wellington Brownies entertain residents at the Cottage Hospital, Christmas 1975.

Wombridge County Primary School visit to the Houses of Parliament, 9th November 1976. The MP for the Wrekin, Gerry Fowler, stands on the right.

Len Murray and his wife pay a visit to the boardroom of the Telford Development Corporation, Priorslee Hall, 2nd February 1974. Mr Murray (later Lord Murray) was born in Hadley and educated at Wellington Grammar School.

John Silkin, Minister for Planning and Local Government, views the beginning of Telford's new town centre from a helicopter, 14th June 1974.

The Duke of Gloucester (in the striped suit) visits the Aerospace Museum, RAF Cosford, 1981.

Prince Bernhard of the Netherlands talks to Station Commander, Group Captain Campbell, RAF Cosford, 19th April 1980.

Sir Keith Joseph (now Lord Joseph) receives a gift after performing the opening ceremony, The Long Warehouse, Coalbrookdale, 1983.

IRON BRIDGE BICENTENARY 1779~1979

Annual Special Constabulary inspection, Wellington Police Station, Autumn 1984.

Princess Anne stops to chat with a young "fall guy" in Telford — ten-year-old Matthew Fall to be precise.

Matthew, from Trench, Shropshire, was among the hundreds who greeted the Princess yesterday.

She arrived by helicopter to open Telford's new £2.5 million Olympic standard ice rink.

Inside little Clare Bennett found meeting a princess is not easy, especially on skates.

She glided across the ice to present the royal visitor with a posy — but had trouble stopping. Lord Northfield, chairman of Telford Development Corporation, came to the aid of the 10-year-old skater.

Putting out his hands he gently caught Clare before she skated into the Princess.

As she declared the rink open Princess Anne said: "I wish everyone who uses it happy landings."

13 11 84

A little girl's big moment. The Queen was obviously delighted by this impromptu presentation as she toured the £100 million shopping development in Telford yesterday.

The Queen was there to open the £50 million second phase of the project.

The phase provides under-cover shopping space, equivalent in size to seven football grounds, and meant the Queen had to walk through around half a mile of crowded, winding shopping corridors.

Security officials searched dozens of shops before the Queen arrived, but police were still posted at many of the shop doorways.

Although the hundreds of well-wishers were held back by barriers, the Queen moved towards them and spoke to many.

A police officer admitted: "It's been a bit of a nightmare."

After opening the centre the Queen left to visit an Army barracks at Tern Hill, near Market Drayton, Shropshire.

The three WRVS ladies, on the left, receive long service medals from Lady Higgs, West Midlands area organiser at the Oakengates office of the WRVS, Oakengates, 1986.

Sod-cutting for the contract start, ten-screen cinema, Telford Town Centre, Tuesday 22nd September 1987.

The Duke of Westminster (right) opens the TSB Bank Training College, Telford, 20th May 1988. The plan of the building forms the letter Y which ties in with the Bank's "Yes" campaign.

In May 1989, staff of Weston Park Enterprises Ltd., celebrate the 25th

The Duke of Edinburgh, Patron of the Aerospace Museum, Cosford, is greeted by John Francis, the Museum manager (right), on his visit to the site in May 1987.

AT WORK

MONDAY, NOVEMBER 29, 1875.

CATALOGUE

OF THE VALUABLE

FARMING STOCK,

IMPLEMENTS OF HUSBANDRY,

NEW AND USEFUL STEAM ENGINE,

BOILER, SHAFTING,

HAY, STRAW, TURNIPS,

AND EFFECTS, WHICH MESSRS.

WALKER & H. J. LLOYD

Will Dispose of by Auction,

ON MONDAY, NOVEMBER 29TH, 1875,

By direction of Mr. JNO. BOULTON, jun., upon premises at the

ELMS FARM, ALBRIGHTON,

NEAR WOLVERHAMPTON.

The Sale to commence at Eleven o'clock in the Morning.

Wolverhampton: W. PARKE, Printer.

GEORGE CRUMP,

BUTCHER,

OPPOSITE WATERLOO TERRACE, BRIDGNORTH,

In view of probable changes, arising from the retirement from business of one or more of the oldest established Butchers in this Town, respectfully solicits the patronage and support of the Nobility, Clergy, Gentry, and Public generally, assuring them that all orders with which they may entrust him shall be executed under his own personal care, and with Meat of such quality and price as shall give complete satisfaction, and ensure to him a continuance of their support.

FRANCIS F. FOXALL,

(LATE FRANCIS FOXALL,)

Builder and Contractor,

WHOLESALE ENGLISH & FOREIGN TIMBER MERCHANT.

Dealer in Broseley and Staffordshire Bricks, Tiles and other Briekkiln Goods.

LONDON PLASTERING AND ROMAN CEMENT.

AGENT FOR THE LILLESHALL LIME COMPANY.

WORKS AND TIMBER YARDS:

UNDERHILL STREET,

BRIDGNORTH.

OFFICES—No. 2, EAST CASTLE STREET.

JUST PUBLISHED.

OCEAN'S LULLABY,

BALLAD WITH CHORUS

Words by E. M. SOUTHWELL.   Music by HORACE B. SOUTHWELL.

Bridgnorth—JOHN SEWELL.   London—HOPWOOD & CREW.

PRICE, 1/6.

The Profits arising from the Sale of the above Song will be given to the BRIDGNORTH INFIRMARY.

1878

Unequalled for Quick Thorough Work

I must leave this day month mum if you don't let me use

THE LATEST SANITARY DISCOVERY

"COMPO" THE SELF WASHER

WASHES EVERYTHING.

1910   MANUFACTORY. DUKINFIELD

Pugh's draper's shop, Dawley, 1910.

31

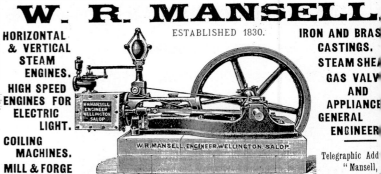

Bakers from Roscoe's Bakery, Finger Road, Dawley, c. 1913.

Horsehay Works Management, c. 1920.

The laundry room, Harper Adams Agricultural College, Edgmond, c. 1933.

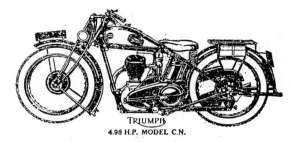

Merrythought Toy Factory, Ironbridge,

The Creamery, Crudgington, 1939.

Dr Crowther, Principal, Harper Adams Agricultural College, Edgmond, oversees the weighing of pig swill, a vital commodity during the Second World War.

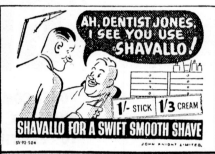

Management and staff, Southwell's Carpet Factory, Bridgnorth, June 1953.

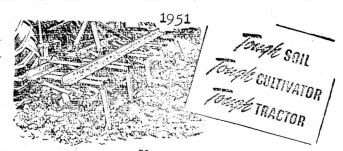

1951

You can cultivate the toughest ground with the Fordson Major Tractor and Fordson Spring Loaded Tine Cultivator. The Major has ample power for the job and the cultivator has all the strength that's needed. Its heavy coil springs allow the tines to over-ride all obstacles safely. It's a 'Precision Built' Fordson Tool Bar Implement. Call, ring or write and ask us for fuller details.

REGINALD TILDESLEY
LIMITED
Main **Fordson** Major Distributors

WILLENHALL   SHIFNAL
121 and 336   Phones   71

FIRED
with
enthusiasm

No more hit or miss firelighting. This is the SURE way—No paper or wood required.
SEE THEM AT YOUR GAS SHOWROOMS

A **GAS** *POKER is so quick*

POKER COMPLETE WITH PLUG-IN TAP AND FLEX INSTALLED AND FITTED TO EXISTING POINT AT HEARTH £1

1955

WEST MIDLANDS GAS BOARD

1956

YOU and **HEINZ**[57] together put 2¼ lb. of tomatoes on the table to enjoy at **every** meal!

Perhaps you didn't realise — it takes 2¼ lb. of the finest sun-ripened tomatoes to make every 12-oz. bottle of Heinz Tomato Ketchup. That's not extravagance either.

Never have tomatoes been put to better use. They are blended, as only Heinz know how, with fine spices, sugar and vinegar. Put Heinz Tomato Ketchup on the table — and enjoy the goodness and flavour of 2¼ lb. of tomatoes at *every* meal. Heinz Tomato Ketchup. 1/4 or 2/-.

Staff at The Red Lion (formerly The Pavilion) on the A5 road, Wellington, are ready to welcome the dinner guests, 1960.

39

 ROAD TRANSPORT INDUSTRY TRAINING BOARD
MOTEC-HIGH ERCALL TELFORD SHROPSHIRE 1971

Coming up for a shower after an arduous shift, Granville Colliery, 29th November 1977.

AT PLAY

Bridgnorth Town F.C., 1899. The team had just beaten Oswestry United Reserves to win the Shropshire Junior Cup.

St Leonard's F.C., Bridgnorth, 1909.

Billy Wright, born in Ironbridge, holds his two-day-old daughter, Victoria, whilst his wife, Joy, looks on, 7th April 1959. With them are the other members of the famous singing trio, the Beverley Sisters, Teddie and Babs. The baby's birth coincided with the announcement that Billy was to gain his 100th soccer cap for England (versus Scotland) four days later.

Wombridge School Football Team, 1951.

Students' cricket team, Harper Adams Agricultural College, Edgmond, c. 1930.

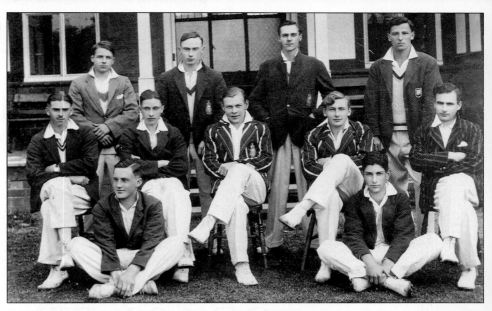

The Harper Adams Agricultural College Tennis Team, Edgmond, c. 1929.

Children at Weston School rehearse for a Physical Display to mark the opening of Shifnal Cottage Hospital by the Countess of Bradford. The hospital was officially opened on 29th July 1939 and closed on 31st July 1991.

Sir Gordon Richards, the racehorse trainer and champion jockey, was born in Donnington Wood on 5th May 1904. In 1947 he rode an incredible 269 winners. He died on 10th November 1986.

Wrekin Golf Club.

WHEN Wellington golfers in 1909 left the old nine-hole course at Steeraway for their present eighteen-hole course on the lower slopes of the Wrekin and Ercall Hills, they decided that the new club should be known by the name of the mountain rather than the town. It was, I think, a particularly happy choice, for the course of the Wrekin Golf Club is in every way typical of mountain golf at its best. We have the exhilarating air that goes with a situation between five and six hundred feet above sea-level. We have magnificent views of the Welsh Hills away to the west, and of Lilleshall, Cannock Chase and a score of minor landmarks close at hand, diversified by delightful unexpected glimpses of wood and valley through odd gaps in the succession of hill-slopes that win in our march. Above all, we have the glorious mountain turf, and the varied contours and natural hazards of the hill country, which provide us with a succession of colourful and adventurous holes. **1938**

The world number two Chess player, Victor Korchnoi, takes part in a simultaneous display, GKN Sankey, Hadley, May 1980. Korchnoi defected from the USSR and played for Switzerland.

Winners of the Group Dwellings Domino League, The Ley, Dawley, 1982.

Travelling from Lilleshall Hall to the Abbey, c. 1933.

Lord Bradford annually inspected Weston School gardens, awarded and presented prizes. Here, the pupils are tending their own plots prior to the judging, 1938.

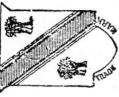
A COUPLE of weeks ago Dora saw an advertisement for a certain book. The ad. said it was hot stuff, so Dora went and bought a copy.

When I met her the other day I asked her what she thought of the book.

"It offended me," she said.

"What! Do you mean to say it was as bad as that?"

"Oh, no! I was offended because it wasn't as bad as the advertisement said it was."

ONLY the sky ould be the limit for these three potential sports super-stars at a West Midlands Guinness School of Sport.

Pictured here are gymnast Judith Davies, 14, from Sutton Coldfield (centre), Amanda Ward 17, England's junior No. 1 squash player, from Birmingham (left), and England under-21 hockey international Janet Horton, 19, from Wichenford, Worcester.

Forty one West Midland youngsters aged between 16 and 21 have been selected for international level training and coaching in fencing, gymnastics, squash, cycling, ski-ing, athletics and hockey in a week-long School of Sport sponsored by the brewery at the Lilleshall National Sports Centre.

The idea is to turn those with outstanding potential into the athletic "super-stars" of tomorrow after specialised and concentrated training at the Shropshire centre. 24.7.77

48

- MEMORANDUM FROM -   1910

The Wright Animated Picture Co.,

(PROPRIETORS :   H. O. & W. I. WRIGHT.)

Mill Bank, Wellington, Salop.

Lessees and Proprietors of

| **GRAND THEATRE.** Wellington. | **PAVILION THEATRE.** Wellington. | **THE PICTURE HOUSE.** Oakengates. | **THE PICTURE HOUSE,** Newport, Salop. |

The Royal cinema, King Street, Dawley, 1939. It first opened in 1937.

PICTURE HOUSE
The Warfage   Ironbridge

Opened April 13th 1912.

Seating 200
3d & 6d (Balcony)

Formerly The Croft School.

Manager Mr. T. Bickley

Mr. Lewis J. Hales is a practical operator and the steadiness of the pictures has been favourably commented upon by the audiences.

The Town Hall cinema, Market Street, Wellington, 1935/6.

1913—1962
The Directors of
WRIGHTS PICTURE HOUSE (NEWPORT) LTD.
REGRET TO ANNOUNCE THAT
THE PICTURE HOUSE, NEWPORT
will CLOSE after the last performance on
SATURDAY, JUNE 30th.

They wish to thank all who have given them their patronage throughout the half-century, including two world wars, during which the Cinema never closed.

"GONE TO EARTH" Most of the filming, of this David O. Selznick version of the Mary Webb novel, was done in and around Much Wenlock, during the summer of 1949. Many local people were featured in the film.

The film's stars were the Hollywood actress, Jennifer Jones (wife of Mr Selznick) and our own, David Farrar, seen here getting to grips with the much-loved character actor, Esmond Knight.

George Cole, one of the supporting players in the film, went on to become one of today's top TV stars.

Working in a time warp as the old meets the new. The "policeman" on the left is really R. A. Winby, an engineer by trade.

Much Wenlock's Town Clerk, A. G. Matthews, with Vivien Knight (the film's publicist) and wholesale fruiterer, E. B. Higgs (left).

Chief continuity girl, Doreen Francis (with stopwatch) and her assistant, Joanne Busby, wait with the villagers for the sun to come out.

Arthur Askey stars in "Make Mine A Million", from Monday onwards, at the Picture House, Newport.

Peter Cushing, starring in the "Hound of the Baskervilles" at the Grand, Wellington, later this week.

CLIFTON WELLINGTON

Phone 439

1959

Sunday, August 2.
JOHN DEREK, JOAN EVANS, "THE FORTUNE HUNTER" (U). Color.
ROD CAMERON, "NIGHT FREIGHT" (U).
Monday, August 3. Matinees: Monday and Tuesday. Three Days.
Greatest Ever Holiday Laughter Show!
DANNY KAYE, MAI ZETTERLING, TORIN THATCHER
"KNOCK ON WOOD" (U). Technicolor. 1.30, 5.00, 8.30.
DEAN MARTIN, JERRY LEWIS,
"LIVING IT UP" (U). Technicolor. 3.15, 6.45.
Last Complete Programme: 6.45. Wednesday: Continuous from 4.45.
Thursday, August 6. Matinee: Saturday. Three Days.
Once... Only once in a lifetime, a Cast... a Story... A Motion Picture like this!
Hecht, Hill and Lancaster present
RITA HAYWORTH, DEBORAH KERR, DAVID NIVEN, WENDY HILLER
and BURT LANCASTER,
"SEPARATE TABLES" (A). 2.45, 5.40, 8.30.
SEAN LYNCH, BETH ROGAN, "INNOCENT MEETING" (A). 1.40, 4.25, 7.20.
Last Complete Programme: 7.15. Thursday and Friday: Continuous from 4.25.

GRAND | GROSVENOR

Wellington Phone 297 | **Oakengates** Phone 48

Sunday, August 2nd.
"NIGHTMARE"
(A) EDWARD G. ROBINSON.
"GHOST TOWN" (U). KENT TAYLOR.

Monday, August 3rd. For Three Days.
Matinees: Monday and Tuesday.
GARY COOPER, MARIA SCHELL,
"THE HANGING TREE" (A).
2.40, 5.25, 8.15.
CHARLES McGRAW, "THE MONEY"
(U). 1.50, 4.35, 7.25.

Thursday, August 6th. For Three Days.
Matinee: Saturday.
PETER CUSHING, CHRISTOPHER LEE
"HOUND OF THE BASKERVILLES"
(A). Colour. 3.15, 5.50, 8.30.
PATRICIA DRISCOLL,
"THE CHILD AND THE KILLER"
(A). 2.05, 4.45, 7.25.

Sunday, August 2nd.
WILLIAM HOLDEN
"SUBMARINE COMMAND" (U).
ROD CAMERON
"PASSPORT TO TREASON" (U).
Monday, August 3rd. For Three Days.
Matinee: Monday.
Monday: Continuous from 2.0; Tuesday and Wednesday: Continuous from 4.40.
NORMAN WISDOM
"THE SQUARE PEG"
3.15, 5.55, 8.35 (U).
JOHN ASHLEY
"FURY UNLEASHED"
2.05, 4.45, 7.25 (U).
Thursday, August 6th. For Three Days.
Matinee: Saturday.
Thursday and Friday, Continuous from 4.55. Saturday, Continuous from 1.40.
The Greatest Submarine Picture Of Them All...
GLENN FORD, ERNEST BORGNINE
"TORPEDO RUN"
(U).
CinemaScope. Colour. 1.55, 5.10, 8.25.
GEORGE NADER
"NOWHERE TO GO"
3.30, 6.45 (U).

MAJESTIC BRIDGNORTH PHONE 3274 An ABC Theatre

August 3. For Six Days. "TOM THUMB" (Tech). (U).
RUSS TAMBLYN, TERRY THOMAS, PETER SELLERS. 2.20, 5.15, 8.15.
"ANDY HARDY COMES HOME" (U). MICKEY ROONEY, FAY HOLDEN, and introducing Mickey's own son, TEDDY ROONEY. 3.50, 6.50. News. Matinee every day from 2 o'clock.
Sunday, August 2. "FOUR GUNS TO THE BORDER" (U). Tech. RORY CALHOUN, GEORGE NADER. 4.40, 7.35.
"KEEP IT CLEAN" (U). RONALD SHINER, JAMES HAYTER. 3.15, 6.5.

ELITE CINEMA, Broseley.
Two Days. Tuesday and Thursday. August 4th and 6th.
"10 NORTH FREDERICK." GARY COOPER, DIANE VARSI.
Also "SHOWDOWN AT BOOT HILL".
Saturday, August 8th "THE TIN STAR", HENRY FONDA, ANTHONY PERKINS.
Also "THE SPANISH AFFAIR."

CENTRAL CINEMA, Ironbridge Tel. Ironbridge 3228
Week Commencing August 2, 1959. Sunday, Monday and Tuesday.
"THE LAW AND JAKE WADE"
PATRICIA OWENS, ROBERT MIDDLETON. Times of Showing: 6.15 and 8.55 p.m.
Also "TARZAN AND THE LOST SAFARI"
Wednesday and Thursday.
"GUN THE MAN DOWN"
JAMES ARNETT, EMILE MEYER. Times of Showing: 7.19 and 9.25 p.m.
Also "WINK OF AN EYE."
Note: Programmes Commence at 6.0 p.m. on each of these two days.
Friday and Saturday.
"MERRY ANDREW", DANNY KAYE, PIER ANGELO.
(Cinemascope and Technicolor). Times of Showing: Friday, 6.0 p.m. and 8.35 p.m.
Saturday, 6.02 and 8.47 p.m. Also "NOTHING BUT TROUBLE"
Note: Programme Commences at 6.0 p.m. on Friday, and 5.0 p.m. on Saturday.

WEM CINEMA
Monday and Tuesday, Aug. 3 and 4.
Matinee: Bank Holiday Monday at 4.45 p.m.
WILLIAM HOLDEN, MACDONALD CAREY and WILLIAM BENDIX.
"STREETS OF LAREDO"
(U). Technicolor)

Friday and Saturday, Aug. 7 and 8.
SHIRLEY EATON, WILFRID HYDE WHITE and TERENCE LONGDON
"CARRY ON NURSE" (U).
Also LEE PATTERSON and HAZEL COURT, "BREAKOUT" (U).

WENLOCK CINEMA
Monday, Aug. 3. For one Day Only.
YUL BRYNNER, MARIA SCHELL and CLAIRE BLOOM
"THE BROTHERS KARAMAZOV"
(A). (Metro Color).

Friday and Saturday, Aug. 7 and 8.
ETHEL MERMAN, VERA ELLEN, DONALD O'CONNOR and GEORGE SANDERS
"CALL ME MADAM" (Technicolor) (U)

PICTURE HOUSE, Newport Tel. Newport 2158.
Monday, August 3rd. For Three Days.
ARTHUR ASKEY in "MAKE MINE A MILLION" (U). 6.20 and 9.10.
Also BARRY FITZGERALD in "BROTH OF A BOY" (U). 7.45.
Thursday, August 6th. For Three Days.
ROBERT TAYLOR, CYD CHARISSE in "PARTY GIRL" (A).
Metrocolor. Cinemascope. 6.45 and 9.0.

The Clifton cinema, Bridge Road, Wellington, 18th May 1963.

53

Bolas Magna Primary School is small. It has 33 pupils, two teachers, and in athletics, the children have to run 34½ laps round the school to the mile.

But last night the 18 junior pupils and 15 infants put on possibly the most ambitious theatrical production of the school's 100 year history.

For the first time in living memory of the 200 inhabitants of the parish of Bolas Magna, the school staged a Nativity play in the tiny parish church of St. John the Baptist, and all 33 pupils were in it. 14.12.76

Production of "Hiawatha", The Hiatt College, Wellington, Summer 1945.

Glenn Miller.

Shropshire Youth Orchestra, conducted by Miss R. Schroeder, 1954. The orchestra was made up of young musicians from all over the county.

55

GOOD music is becoming a glut on the ether.

While most people in the concert-going world are hailing the B.B.C. as a new Fairy Godmother, many hundreds of thousands of mere wireless listeners are finding cause for nightly annoyance in the methods employed in broadcasting the more serious musical programmes.

For the past six weeks the Promenade concerts from the Queen's Hall have been a vast joy to a few hundreds in London, but an insufferable bore to countless Average Listeners who tune in after dinner hoping for a little entertainment.

This is partly due to the laziness of the Average Listener in not taking the trouble to pay proper attention to what he is supposed to be listening to, but largely the fault of Savoy-hill, who throw on to the air enormous doses of music without the slightest explanation.

You turn the knob and listen to what may be Beethoven, or may be Mahler, or may—if your set is bad—be Mozart. Sometimes it is necessary to wait half an hour to solve the riddle.

An Elgar Mystery.

This is a very short-sighted policy on the part of the B.B.C., and one calculated to hinder Mrs. Philip Snowden's worthy "make-good-music-popular-with-the-people" policy.

At a concert no one dreams—if they haven't the actual orchestral score on their knee—of not using the extensive analytical programmes supplied. Even

then one has the conductor to look at, and the actual sight of the players to guide one in following the music. But to the wireless listener all this is denied.

The other night Elgar's Symphony No. 2 in E flat was broadcast from the Queen's Hall, the audience being "requested to refrain from applause between the movements of the symphony."

A friend of mine listened in to this particular item for twenty-five minutes. He had not the vaguest idea what it was, but was increasingly fascinated with the general magnificence of the music.

Was it necessary to conceal the meaning of the four movements from the blind listener?   1930

Week-End High Spots

Good morning, Everybody!

THE abnormal situation has upset the programme arrangements of the B.B.C., owing to the using of the Regional transmitters for special news bulletins to Continental countries.

I was hoping that we might have gone back to normal working to-day, but we must be content with a National programme, and another to cover all the Regional transmitters.

★   ★   ★

EVEN though the foreign news broadcasts are continuing this week-end, there will be much more tranquillity about our listening to radio than we have experienced during the past few days.

We cannot exactly make merry with the fare offered, but there are periods when we can relax and thoroughly enjoy what is offered.

National provides sport, dance music, variety, Reggie Foort, a real Harvest Home on a Wiltshire farm, and some

special dance music from Chicago which will provide comparison with our best rhythm band.

★   ★   ★

ON the Regionals there will be a relay of Puccini's opera "La Bohème" from Streatham Hill Theatre, and other excellent music, principally of the lighter type.

Television, too, provides an excellent programme for the Home Counties.

Two shows for to-morrow will be more interesting than listening to advertisements.

National gives us the light opera, "Tom Jones," and Regionals "Barnum—the Greatest Show on Earth." This should have been on the air some weeks ago, but had to be postponed.

Happier week-end listening will be the opportunity of most broadcast fans.

1938
Grid Leak.

Today's TV and radio
5.9.60

I.T.A.

ASSOCIATED TELEVISION

5.0 Seeing Sport: Football. 5.25 The Adventures of Popeye.

5.55 News. 6.5 Midlands News. 6.10 Who Goes Next?— Malcolm Muggeridge and Harold Wilson, M.P. 6.30 Abbott and Costello Show: "In Society."

7.0 Rainbow Room—with Jean Morton and Peter Cavanagh. 7.30 Criss Cross Quiz.

8.0 Michael Medwin in "The Love of Mike." 8.30 Bonanza: "The Philip Diedesheimer Story."

9.25 News. 9.35 Deadline Midnight—last story in the series concerns a financier and his missing son.

10.35 Alan Taylor's weekly lecture on "Prime Ministers of England"—Gladstone. 11.5 News Headlines. 11.7 Midland Farming. 11.22 Epilogue.

B.B.C.

5.0 Olympic Games. 5.30 Summerhouse, a seasonal programme.

6.0 News and weather. 6.10 Midland News. 6.20 My Word! (panel game).

6.50 Tonight. 7.29 Headline News. 7.30 Tony Hancock in The Best of Hancock: "The Big Night."

8.0 Panorama—people, places and problems in the news. 8.45 "Here lies Miss Sabry" (mystery serial—part 5).

9.15 Philip Marlowe: Philip Carey in Death Takes a Lover. 9.40 News. 9.55 Greyhound St. Leger at the Empire Stadium, Wembley.

10.10 Olympic Games (Boxing). 10.55 News. 11.0 Olympic Games.—(continued). 12.0 Weather.

Sound

MIDLAND HOME SERVICE. — 5.0 Children's Hour: "The Carved Lions." 5.30 Our Garden. 5.55 Weather. 6.0 News. 6.15 Midland News. 6.30 Sport. 6.40 Signpost. 7.0 Johnny's Journey, 1960 (Johnny Morris—Greece).

7.30 Promenade Concert. 9.0 News. 9.15 Promenade Concert (part 2). 10.0 "Dear Miss Prior," a play from the novel by W. M. Thackeray. 11.0 News. 11.6-11.36 Music at Night.

LIGHT PROGRAMME. — 4.45 Sam Costa's Record Rendezvous. 5.30 Roundabout. 6.29 Olympic Games. 6.42 Tonight's Topic. 6.45 The Archers. 7.0 Radio Newsreel. 7.25 Sport. 7.30 Mr. Piano Plays (Joe Henderson).

8.0 A Night at the Varieties (old-time music hall). 8.30 True Story: "How I Survived," by Bob Kesten. 9.0 Jack Jackson's Record Roundabout. 10.15 Olympic Games. 10.30 News. 10.40 String along. 11.55-12.0 News.

NETWORK THREE AND THIRD PROGRAMME. — 6.40 Talking about the Proms. 7.10 Russian by Interview. 7.30 Chess.

8.0 Robert Eddison in "The Green Bay Tree," by Edouard Dujardin. 9.15 Piano Recital by Else Cross. 9.45 The Future Guardians—a portrait of African leadership by Erskine B. Childers. 10.45 Dennis Brain Wind Ensemble.

11.6-11.11 Market Trends.

RADIO LUXEMBOURG. — 7.0 Non-Stop Pops. 7.30 Requests. 8.30 Date with Perry Como. 8.45 Pops at the Piano. 9.0 Red Nichols and his Five Pennies. 9.15 Jo Stafford Show. 9.45 Lonely Man. 10.0 Top Pops. 10.30 Hit Parade. 11.0 Spin with the Stars. 11.15 Your Record Date. 11.30 World Tomorrow. 12.0 Search the Scriptures. 12.15-12.30 Music at Bedtime.

Jo Stafford, Radio Luxembourg, 9.15 pm.

Tony Hancock, who can be seen on BBC TV tonight at 7.30 p.m.

20th December 1977   Oakengates Town Hall

Programme

OVERTURE: THE NEW DAY SOUND

Your compere . . .

ALTON DOUGLAS

introducing

NORMA LEON

****

VINCE EAGER

****

RICHARD CROMWELL

I N T E R V A L
(approx. 15 minutes)

ALTON DOUGLAS

introducing

Star of T.V. and Radio

TOM O'CONNOR

Nicholas Witchell, one of the BBC Breakfast News team, born in Cosford.

OUT & ABOUT

A GUIDE
TO THE
WREKIN
AND ITS ENVIRONS: 1879
INCLUDING
Descriptive Notes

"One touch of Nature makes the whole World kin"

Ironbridge, c. 1885.

The Post Office and Coffee Palace, Oakengates, 1893.

The Market Place, Oakengates, 1895.

The Wrekin, from Buckatree Hall, Wellington, 1889.

Jackfield, at the turn of the century.

The Crown Inn, High Street, Albrighton, near Cosford, 1905.

Weston Village Pump, 1906.

The River Severn at Buildwas, looking towards Benthall Edge, 1912.

Wellington, from above Ercall Quarry, The Wrekin, 1912.

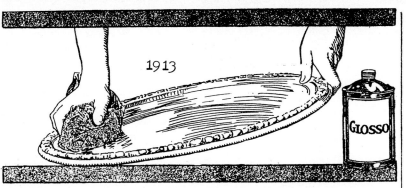

1913

You can get a shine in
half the time with 'GLOSSO'

Such a shine too. It only takes *half the time* and *labour* that ordinary polishes do. Glosso stops at nothing; no matter how dirty or how neglected your metal is, a few drops and a few brisk rubs will get you a shine such as you can *never* get with ordinary polishes. If you have not tried it yet, write to-day for a

FREE SAMPLE

Sent post paid on receipt of a post card bearing your own *and your dealer's* name and address to Dept. J 23

HARGREAVES BROS. & CO. LTD.

The 'Gipsy Black Lead' People.

HULL.

GLOSSO

THE ONE-MINUTE METAL POLISH

Sold by Grocers, Oilmen and Stores in 1/-, 6d., 3d. and 2d. waste-preventing tins.

DANGER
1916

Danger from infectious disease is averted in

EVERY
BRITISH HOME

by constant use of

FIRST AID

THE MODERN
DISINFECTANT SOAP

A Useful Chart of **FIRST AID HINTS** *with illustrations sent free on application to the makers of* First-Aid Soap, CHRISTR. THOMAS & BROS. LTD. Broad Plain, BRISTOL.

Used in military hospitals and recommended by medical men.

HAVE YOUTHFUL HAIR!

Grey Hair Will No Longer Rob You of Your Youthful Looks If You Try This Simple Home Recipe.

If your hair has begun to turn grey, or has a faded, lustreless appearance, you can readily darken it and bring back its beauty by using this home recipe, which is neither expensive or difficult to prepare. In half-a-pint of water mix these ingredients, to be had at any chemists.

Bay Rum ....1 oz.
Orlex Compound.................1 small box.

This preparation is also fine for the scalp, allays all itching, removes dandruff and stops falling hair. Apply once a day until the hair is darkened, then once every two weeks will be sufficient. Be sure the chemist gives you Orlex Compound, for no substitute will give the same good results.—(Advt.)   *1916*

HINTS FOR THE HOME.

MARGARINE AND BUTTER.

Margarine is no longer the despised and suspected product of pre-war days. The best brands are known, says a writer in the *Woman at Home*, to be made under conditions which are as good as, if not superior to, those under which butter is made, and many people declare a preference for the best quality margarine for table use to a second quality butter.

Its tastelessness and a certain oiliness were, in the early days, the objections to the use of this substitute, and also a belief that in nutritive power it was behind butter. This has been proved ancient history. The usual brands of margarine are made from nuts, palm oils, animal fats, or dairy products, and are in themselves as good and nutritive and palatable articles of food as butter.

The melting-point of some of the nut butters is different from that of butter and dripping, and is not suitable for frying; but in practice others will be found quite good, though there does not seem much need for its use for this purpose save in the case of omelettes or such things. In pastry-making even the cheap margarines are found to give good results, and to be as light as butter and better than cooking butter.

The relation of their nutritive power is simply expressed by saying most butters contain 89 per cent. of fat and most margarine 80 per cent. With this slight difference a comparison of their prices is instructive. In pastry-making two-thirds of the quantity of margarine is sufficient, thus effecting an even greater economy.   *29.7.16*

Reg Gower and his mum wait to go for a spin in the family Austin Seven, High Rock, Listley Street, Bridgnorth, 1924.

High Rock, taken from River Fields, Bridgnorth, 1923.

Darley's Landing Place, Bridgnorth, c. 1925.

High Street and Market Square, Bridgnorth, c. 1925.

The Black Lion Hotel, Hilton, c. 1930.

AN ELECTRIC HOT-WATER JUG

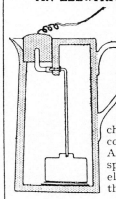

A LIDLESS pot in the form of a jug, mug, or jar is made of insulating material and has a top plate from which a heating device is suspended. This device comprises grooved plates carrying resistances, this being mechanically and electrically connected by a metal rod. A plug which fits into the spout is linked with the electric supply which heats the liquid in the jug. *1930*

A USEFUL SHOVEL

IT is always an inconvenience when using a shovel if one wants to leave it temporarily to have to find a wall or post to rest it against, or to lay it down on the ground. In the shovel shown in the picture the handle is pivoted. When not in use the shovel can be left in the position shown, the handle standing upright. When using it the handle fits into a groove and is held by a clip, becoming thus the ordinary type of shovel. The clip which holds the end of the handle in position consists of a metal spring, so that it requires no fastening or adjustment.

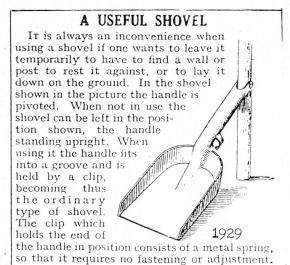

1929

Madeley Wood, Ironbridge, from the south side of the Severn, August 1930.

Weston Hall and Park, c. 1935.

FASHIONS
FOR THE OLDER WOMAN
cleverly designed and cut to disguise those "extra inches"

A FROCK in patterned silk with a loose but well-cut coat to match, makes an ideal summer outfit. On the left is a charming design (No. 9,731) which takes 7¾ yds. of 36-in. material in the 40-in. bust size, or if you should prefer to make the coat of a contrasting colour, buy 4 yds. for the frock and 3¾ yds. for the coat.

Frock and Coat No. 9,731. 40-50 in. bust sizes. Pattern price 1s. 6d.

P LAIN shantung silk was chosen for the simple beach frock on the right (No. 9,679) with its tri-angular pockets and panels at back and front of the skirt. In the 40-in. bust size you'll need 4¼ yds. of 36-in. material.

(Below) Frock No. 9,623. 10-16 years. Bargain Pattern. Price 4½d.

OUR BARGAIN PATTERN

D IAGONALLY - CHECKED " Tobralco " makes this neat little frock for that schoolgirl daughter of yours, with its stitched neck, belt and front trimmings. Allow 2¼ yds. of 36-in. material for the 10-12 years' size, 2¾ yds. for the 12-14 years' size, and 3¼ yds. for the 14-16 years' size. Send to the address on this page, marking your envelope " Bargain Pattern," and enclosing the coupon cut from below.

Frock No. 9,675. 40-50 in. bust sizes. Pattern price 1s.

A NOTHER simply-made frock is No. 9,675 (shown above), this time with a round neck and pleats at the front of the skirt. Choose a striped silk for this design, and buy 4¼ yds. of 36-in. material for the 40-in. bust size.

WOMAN'S OWN BARGAIN PATTERN COUPON
No. 9,623
10-12, 12-14 or 14-16 years' sizes
June 5, 1937

Frock No. 9,679. 40-50 in. bust sizes. Pattern price 1s.

HOW TO ORDER
Hand-cut patterns of designs shown on this page can be obtained, post free, at the prices stated either from the Pattern Shop, "Woman's Own," Tower House, Southampton Street, Strand, London, W.C.2, or by overseas readers from overseas agents at same price. Be careful to state the correct size of patterns, as they cannot be exchanged. Also note that quantities of material given here are for the sizes mentioned only. The others are given in the leaflets which we send with the patterns.

Preparing for Maypole dancing, Wombridge, 1934.

JUST A THOUGHT

Water Imps

I SAW in the heart of town the children out of school floating little paper boats upon a muddy pool. It might have been a lido from the sunshine on their faces, and I have seen less fun at much more fashionable places. They paddled and they splashed, they raced their boats with one another, and many a muddy sock went home to many an anxious mother.

Be it a puddle or a pond, the ocean or a stream—water is a mother's worry and the children's dream.

— KATHLEEN PARTRIDGE

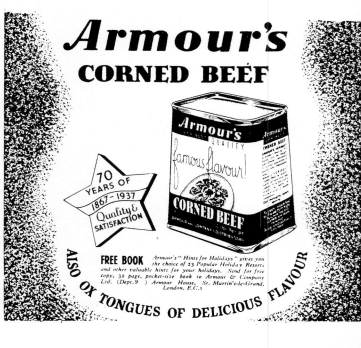

A game of rounders for the girls of Weston School, c. 1935.

- whilst the boys enjoy their cricket.

Doseley Church, 1943. It is now used as a private residence.

Bell P-39 Airacobras of the American Air Force at Atcham, July 1943. Long-range belly-tanks were fitted to the aircraft prior to flights to North Africa.

FOOD FACTS

Thank the farmer—
bless the weather—
1943

for plenty of green vegetables *NOW!*

A mild season has advanced the crops — that's why health-giving green vegetables are top-of-the-bill this week. Make the most of them while they last! We all need all the Vitamin C we can get, *and* more variety in our diet. Make cabbage a "special" tonight. Make greenstuffs a daily "extra" while they stay plentiful and cheap. It's nothing but common sense to go for the good things while they are at their cheapest and most abundant. So fill up your shopping basket at the greengrocer's!

4 RULES FOR COOKING GREEN VEGETABLES

1 Don't soak green vegetables before cooking. Wash them thoroughly in cold salted water.

2 Cook them as quickly as possible.

3 Use only enough water to keep pan from burning. A teacupful is usually enough.

4 Bring water to the boil, put in shredded greens, put the lid on the pan and cook steadily for 10 to 15 minutes. Give the pan a shake once or twice during that time. Serve at once.

LISTEN TO
THE KITCHEN FRONT
EVERY MORNING AT 8.15

> **National Milk Scheme.**
> **Important**
>
> Apply to the Food Office this week for authorities for free or 2d. milk for expectant mothers, and free milk for children holding R.B.2 (green book). Take or send the ration book when you apply. Expectant mothers must also produce medical certificate. R.B.2 holders not eligible for free supplies of liquid milk need not apply.

THE MINISTRY OF FOOD, LONDON, W.I. FOOD FACTS NO. 135

Admaston, 1947.

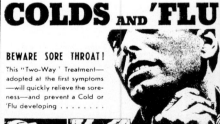

74

Sixth Form, with headmaster, Mr Jakeman, Bridgnorth Grammar School (now the Endowed School), 13th June 1946.

High Street, Much Wenlock, June 1950.

THE ONLY PUBLIC CLOCK in Oakengates. Local records—and memories—have been searched without success to discover who owns it. Mr. Richard Pinks, clerk to the Urban Council, wants to know because the council wants to get it repaired. The town wants it repaired because workers have said it never showed the right time, and has made them miss buses. The Conservative Party is among those who rent rooms below the clock, which is kept going by Mr. Stanley New. "As it now badly needs cleaning," Mr. Pinks told a representative of *The Birmingham Post* last night, "we shall have to decide at our next meeting what to do about it."

FOUR men and a woman from the "doomed" Shropshire village of Jackfield, which is partly slipping into the River Severn, yesterday won a reprieve for 170 villagers whom officials want to evacuate and rehouse.

Officials at a conference of local authorities and public services claimed it would be "unpracticable" to try to stop the landslide which has ruined six houses, threatens 24 more, and may isolate 50 others through the collapse of the village's only road.

But the villagers replied: "We don't want to leave our houses. Find the cure for our landslide, and we will help to pay."

The conference, held in the Town Hall at nearby Broseley, agreed that a county council committee should call on the country's greatest experts—the Department of Scientific and Industrial Research—for a pilot survey to find the cause of the slipping, and see if there may be a cure.

CHEAPER TO REHOUSE 24.4.52

Reports from the Ministry of Works, British Railways and the county surveyor said the subsidence was due to flooding of old clay and coal pits under the village.

"I should say," said the surveyor, Mr. G. C. Cowie, "that the area is doomed and the only practicable solution is to rehouse on a more stable site."

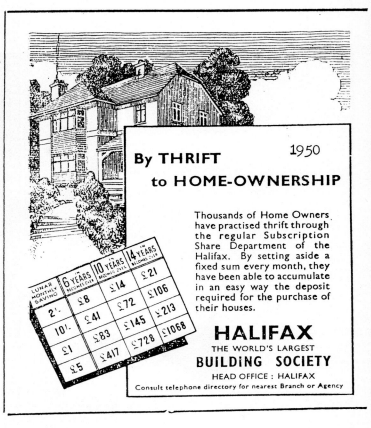

"This is how it works", The Creamery, Crudgington, 1959.

Dawley, June 1953.

Admaston, 1955.

Low Town, Bridgnorth, 1963. St Mary's School (foreground) now demolished. The Well Meadow Estate not yet built.

Oakengates, May 1963.

Lightmoor Halt, 1963. It was close to Lightmoor rail-junction and has since been demolished.

Wellington railway shed, with two Pannier Tank engines, 1964.

Park Avenue, Madeley, 8th December 1964.

High Street, Ironbridge, July 1965.

Midday in Ironbridge, July 1965..

Mr. Keith Beddoes, the man who first thou ght of reopening the Severn Valley line, standing on the footbridge at Bridgnorth Station.

The new steam age is near

AS the first steamless decade begins on main railway routes, steam engine passenger train services are about to return on the 4½ miles of picturesque Severn Valley track from Bridgnorth to Hampton Loade.

This has been made possible by a group of Midland "do-it-yourself" railway enthusiasts who formed them selves into

Evening Mail Reporter

the Severn Valley Railway Company.

The enthusiasts intend to be professionals at running a railway line and at the same time preserve one of their great loves—the steam engine.

V.I.P.s, including a Ministry of Transport inspector, on an informal visit were given a preview at Bridgnorth Station over the weekend of rolling stock waiting to go in action.

The final signal to start operating is expected from Whitehall within a few weeks when the Minister of Transports signs a transfer order.

The reality of this section of the Severn Valley line reopening will be a red letter day in the life of 31-year-old Mr. Keith Beddoes, a maintenance fitter at a Kidderminster carpet factory. He is the man who started it all.

But for Mr. Beddoes writing to a Kidderminster weekly paper, trains would never have returned to the valley.

A railway enthusiast since

boyhood, he became concerned at the closing of lines for economy purposes. He told his brother and two workmates: "Wouldn't it make a nice change to reopen a local railway line?" They agreed and encouraged him to write to the local paper.

Publication resulted in a meeting of 50 railway enthusiasts at a Kidderminster hotel and the Severn Valley Railway Society was formed.

That was in July, 1965. Now, the 1,750 - member - strong "Society" is a properly constituted company housing 11 steam locomotives and more than 20 carriages at Bridgnorth Station, where the line, which originally opened in 1862, was closed by British Rail in 1963.

The green light for the company to run passenger trains came recently when Salop County Council's Road and Bridges Committee withdrew its main objection to the reopening of the line on the grounds the railway would inflate road improvement costs. 1970

The Government gave the green light for the creation of a Southampton-sized city in Shropshire — planned to eventually take 100,000 overspill from Birmingham and the Black Country.

But the Minister of Housing and Local Government, Mr. Anthony Greenwood, pulled a surprise out of the go-ahead package. It should, he insisted, be called Telford after the famous road, bridge and canal builder who had many associations with Shropshire.

Until then it had been assumed that the new era — an enlargement of Dawley New Town to take in Wellington and Oakengates — would be called Wrekin; the name recommended by the public inquiry which looked into the plan.

Alderman Sir Frank Price, Chairman of Dawley Development Corporation, said on hearing the news: "It gives us an opportunity of building a fine large city in the middle of this area." 1968

Apprentice Guard of Honour, inspected by Air Vice-Marshal J.H. Hunter-Tod, RAF Cosford, 24th June 1969.

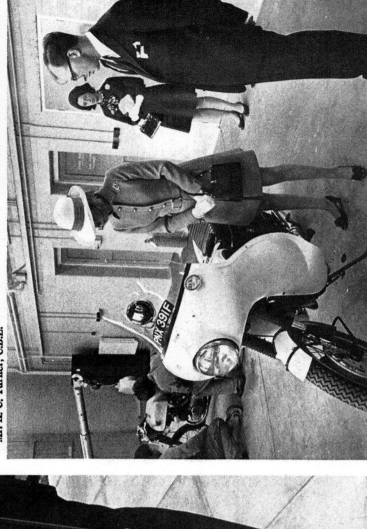

Her Royal Highness enjoying the "drive past" of the MOTEC 1 and group training vehicles depicting the training needs of the road transport industry and the activities undertaken to meet those needs. Seated on her right is the Chairman of the Board, Mr. K. C. Turner, C.B.E.

The range of vehicles within the scope of the Board is extremely wide, including motor cycles, as the Princess had explained to her by the Training Manager, Mr. S. F. Lyne during this section of the tour.

A ceremony pleasantly performed. Here the Princess Anne has just unveiled this stainless steel steering wheel as a record of the occasion. The inscription reads "Her Royal Highness The Princess Anne officially opened MOTEC 1 for the Road Transport Industry Training Board, 10th September, 1969." High Ercall.

Sylvia Martin, of Donnington, seen in the gateway to the north end of Newport, 27th August 1972. In the centre are Beaumaris House and Roddam House.

Where it all started! The Telford Town Centre "green field" site before building begins, 17th July 1970.

Wellington, in the rain, February 1974.

Cutting a Trefoil to celebrate the 60th Anniversary of Guides and Brownies, Methodist Church, Wellington, October 1974.

After the rain. Shawbirch Road, with the Pheasant Inn in the centre, Admaston, 1975.

Telford Town Centre's Mall No. 1 draws the customers in 1974 ....

........and continues to do so in the new Phase 2 in 1982.

High Street, Dawley, 1976.

An anti-litter poster competition, Dothill Infants' School, 1977.

Val adds style to the old valuables

PRETTY Val Robinson was the only thing making temperatures rise in the old forge at Aston Hall, Claverley, Shropshire, yesterday.

For the 6ft. bellows and anvils have not been used since the last blacksmith, Charles Morris, worked there before the First World War.

Yesterday, curio hunters and farmers queued up to bid for lots dating back almost 100 years in the sale of the century.

Far implements, hoof stones, cider flagons and copper fire marks, issued by the Norwich Union as an indication of house insurance in the days when fire brigades had to be paid, all went under the hammer.

23.7.78

High Street, Dawley, 1978.

THE IRONBRIDGE
TELFORD, SHROPSHIRE, ENGLAND
HAS BEEN DESIGNATED AN
HISTORICAL LANDMARK BY
AMERICAN SOCIETY FOR METALS

THE FIRST IRON BRIDGE, CAST OF IRON SMELTED
WITH COKE, ERECTED IN 1779, SYMBOLIZES
PIONEERING METALLURGICAL ACCOMPLISHMENTS,
LEADING TO BRITAIN'S RENOWN FOR ENGINEERING
AND MANUFACTURING INNOVATIONS.

1984

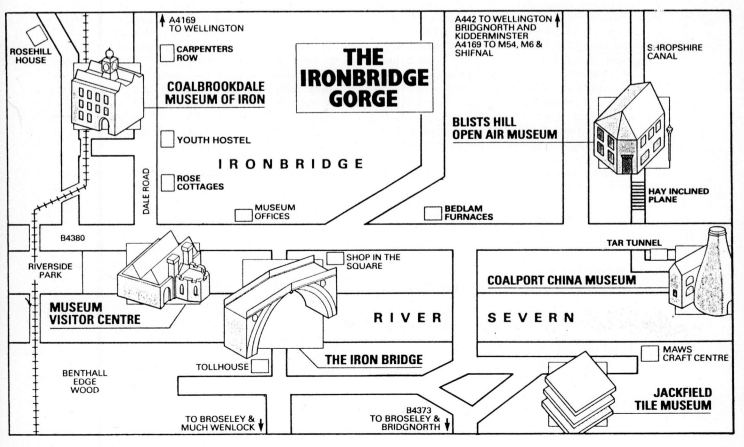

Wem Best Bitter

Salop's own brew

ACKNOWLEDGEMENTS

(for providing photographs, for encouragement and numerous other favours)

Tony Adams; Aerospace Museum, Cosford; Neil Allen; John Ayre; Jean Barrowclough; Bee Cee Enterprises; Richard Bifield; Birmingham Post and Mail Ltd.; Jim Boulton; Fred Brown; Buckatree Hall Hotel; Nick Burch; Dave Carpenter; Coalbrookdale & Ironbridge C. of E. (Aided) Primary School; Commission for the New Towns; Don Cox; Alan and Brenda Cronshaw; Dairy Crest Ingredients; Jim Dutton; Ellerdine County Primary School; Peter Forrest; John Francis; Sheila Gallagher; Reg Gower; Rae Green; Harper Adams Agricultural College, Edgmond; Marian Head; Julie Hill; Chris Huss; Anne Jennings; Dave and Thelma Jones; Ketley County Infants School; Lilleshall National Sports Centre; Terry Lowe; Chris Maddocks; John Marcham; Gill Meredith; Merrythought Ltd.; MOTEC; John Nicholson; Wendy Nicholson; Betty Parker; John Parkes; Ian Pride; Geof Proffitt; RAF, Cosford; Salvation Army; Severn Valley Railway; Carol and Fred Shenton; Beryl and John Shirley; Shropshire Star; Alwin Smith; TSB Training College, Telford; Joan Wanty; Frank Weavers; West Mercia Constabulary, Telford; Weston Park Enterprises Ltd.; Sybil and Trevor Whitmore; Maureen Williams; Barbara and John Wilson; Wombridge County Primary School; Wrekin Council Tourism Office; WRVS.

Please forgive any possible omissions. Every effort has been made to include all organisations and individuals involved in the book.

Back Cover:

Top: Map, showing approximate area covered by the book.

Centre: Wellington Fire Brigade, c. 1895.

Bottom: Andre Wallace's sculpture of Thomas Telford being fixed in place, Civic Square, Telford Centre, March 1988.